The Fruitful Season
Meditations for the Autumn of life

HELEN WARD SCHMIEDER

MOREHOUSE PUBLISHING

Morehouse Publishing
P.O. Box 1321
Harrisburg, PA 17105

Morehouse Publishing is a division of the Morehouse Group.

Printed in the United States of America

Cover design by Trude Brummer

Library of Congress Cataloging-in-Publication Data
Schmieder, Helen Ward, 1927-
    The fruitful season: meditations for the autumn of life/Helen Ward Schmieder.l
    p.cm.
    ISBN 0-8192-1744-1 (pbk.)
    1. Aged—Religious life.   2. Meditations.   I. Title.
BV4580.S32   1998
242'.65—dc21

        98-23401
        CIP

To the sacred memory of our son

David Ward Schmieder
1956–1976

Introduction

Let the words of my mouth and the meditation of my heart be acceptable to you, O LORD, my Rock and my Redeemer.
                                                    Psalm 19:14

How many of us, forty or fifty years ago, would have believed that we would be having a love affair when we were over sixty years old? As you read these meditations I pray you will know that your love affair is with God and that it will grow and grow.

The year before my seventieth birthday I began to think about what I could write for some of my college friends who were also nearing seventy. I wanted to write something special to celebrate their individual birthdays. I wanted to stress the importance of loving God in everyday situations. Since I knew we were all active in our churches, I decided a book of meditations might reflect some of my thoughts. So I wrote "Heavenly Seventy—A Love Affair." My friends received copies and I gave some to other friends who were in their sixties, seventies, and eighties. From their comments I knew the meditations might help the over-sixty crowd. After I contacted Morehouse Publishing and talked to the wonderful editors there, *The Fruitful Season: Meditations for the Autumn of Life* came into being.

The autumn of life is a joyful time. There are many blessings for which we can be grateful, as well as many challenges that we must face. One of the blessings is that we have more time. More time to enjoy our adult children and, of course, our grandchildren. We can take vacations whenever we please. We can continue our physical activities—walking, bicycling, playing tennis, swimming, golfing, or whatever appeals to us—and we have the leisure time with which to pursue them. There is also time to pursue old or new hobbies. For instance, someone I know made model airplanes when he was young. For years he couldn't find the time to continue this hobby, but now that he is retired he has resumed it.

There are also the challenges. We are confronted with the wrinkles and skin blemishes that come with our age. We may have cataracts, false teeth, or hearing aids. Sometimes we have difficulty remembering names or even what was told to us a few hours earlier. But we have the capabilities to accept any challenge.

However, it is hard for us to accept all of the changes in the world around us. Did you know of any couples who lived together when you were in your late teens? Did you ever hear about abortions in those days? How about HIV? Assisted suicide, gene therapy, or organ transplants were not even imagined.

As a rule, when we were married and had children, mothers stayed home with the kids. There were no child-care facilities. If we had appointments or wanted a day out, we left our children with a baby-sitter, neighbor, or relatives. As I look back, it seems that our lives were very simple. It is no wonder that we think the families of today are different.

Even our churches seem to be changing. This can bother us a great deal. We are often very set in our ways and it is difficult to look at new ideas from another perspective. But, believe it or not, after we get used to a new liturgy or worship style, we may be surprised to find that it is very satisfying to us.

Some of us think we know exactly what is wrong with our society today. And we think we know how to cure all of its problems. We think that what worked for us will work for today's generation. Sometimes this is not true, and we are challenged to accept that fact and do the best we can to be helpful. No doubt there are many of us who need a little more patience in solving problems. We have gained some wisdom in our lives, but now we are faced with knowing when to use that wisdom. Sometimes it can be passed on to help others draw closer to God.

The fruitful years are indescribable—what a joy to be in love with a wonderful God who accepts us as we are. What other blessing do we need? What other challenge is more pertinent than sharing God's love with the entire world?

While writing these meditations I felt that God was helping me to reach out to you, my readers. Some of the meditations are about prayer, growing older, retirement, anger, judgment, and God's goodness. It is my hope that the meditations will strengthen you as you continue in your love affair with God. May God continue to bless you as you do his work.

Get a Life!

"I am the way and the truth and the life. No one comes to the Father except through me."

John 14:6

I have been hearing the expression "Get a life" more and more. One of the people I heard talking about it was upset because a friend dwelled on some negative happenings in her life. It seemed that telling her to "Get a life" was meant to give her incentive to change her perspective on life. A friend whose husband had died several months ago told me she was ready to "get a life." She felt she needed to have a different lifestyle now that she was a widow.

We have only one life on earth and we are all capable of using it to follow the teachings of God. What can we do to fulfill our lives? And how can we help others to find fulfillment? There are many drug addicts who need help. There are many alcoholics who need direction. And there are groups that can help them get a life.

Can you think of others who need our help? Consider the children who seldom see their parents from the time they go to school in the morning until they come home at night. Would an after-school program be helpful to them? Single mothers need special encouragement. And what about dropouts from high school?

Let's try to remember that God loves all of us and our lives should reflect that we are trying to love everyone in the world.

Dear God,
We know that our lives are in your hands. We will strive to remember that you, and you alone, are the way and the truth and the life. Amen.

Are You Elderly?

"Is wisdom with the aged, and understanding in length of days?"
Job 12:12

Every so often one sees reports about elderly people being in accidents, and then their age is listed as something like sixty-two. This really drives me crazy since I don't consider myself elderly even at the age of seventy. Do you? Just to be sure, I consulted a dictionary and found that elderly means between middle and old age and pertains to persons in later life. That's us, much as we hate to admit it.

Yet there are rewards for those of us the world considers elderly. Our wisdom and understanding are increasing now that we have more time to learn. Many communities offer adult education classes. It can be very rewarding to take an interesting course. I never knew how to weave baskets, so I took a basket-weaving course. Now I have a new hobby. I noticed that there were many older men and women taking dancing classes. What fun they were having!

At one time I wondered what I was offering to a church group to which I had been elected. My minister told me my wisdom was valuable to the group. Have you noticed that your wisdom seems to grow and grow?

Let's try to think positively, just as God thinks positively about us. We don't think of God as an elderly God. In his sight we are mere youngsters. We may think that we have known God for a long time, yet we are really just beginning to know him. The knowledge of God in our love affair grows stronger every minute.

Rejoice in being elderly.

Dear God,
Your wisdom and understanding are beyond our belief. We need your help in using our own wisdom and understanding to make this world a better place in which to live. Amen.

Are You Lonely?

"The one who sent me is with me; he has not left me alone, for I always do what is pleasing to him."

John 8:29

S ometimes it is good to think about the reasons we are lonely and feel alone. We miss special friends who have moved away or who seem to have forgotten us. If there has been a death of a loved one, we are always going to miss that person.

Many times we feel particularly alone when we are under stress. Or perhaps this is the first time we have ever lived alone. We may get so absorbed with our own problems that we ignore what is going on around us. This can quickly lead to loneliness.

What can we do?

Remember that God is always with us. He is always at our side. We know that Jesus needed to be alone at times, and it may be good for us to follow his example and also to be by ourselves at times.

There are many ways that God helped lonely people. Mary, the mother of Jesus, must have been lonely during her pregnancy. But God was with her all the time, just as he is with us.

When we are lonely, would it help to become involved in volunteering? If we keep busy helping others, we are less apt to feel alone. I am told that people our age who volunteer at schools are never lonely because they think about the children so much. I know that God could never think about his children too much. How great it is to be having a love affair with him.

Dear God,
Help all of the lonely people in the world to feel your presence. Let them feel your love and the love of all your people when they are alone. Amen.

Are You Hungry?

"Blessed are those who hunger and thirst for righteousness, for they will be filled."

Matthew 5:6

We know there are many starving people in the world today. We also know there are many groups that come to the aid of these hungry people. In our country many people our age are involved in soup kitchens, where those without food can get some nourishment.

Do you ever think about the millions of people who hunger for more than food? Every day we rub shoulders with people who are hungry to hear more about the Word of God. We can help ourselves and others to satisfy that kind of hunger by showing God's love to everyone we see in our daily lives.

Would it be helpful to invite these people to go to church with us? Maybe they are interested in attending a Bible study group. Or could a meditation book satisfy their hunger? Perhaps being friendly and caring is food for their hungry souls. Are we really aware of those who hunger and thirst?

All of us need to use our God-given gifts to spread God's word throughout the world. Only then will the hungry be satisfied. Remember that Christ told us he is the bread of life (John 6:48). Take time today to think about what you can do to help feed those who are hungry.

Dear God,
Every day we thank you for giving us food to satisfy our hunger. We know that you are always with us as we learn more about your love. Help us to share that love with others. Amen.

Conscience

Create in me a clean heart, O God, and put a new and right spir-it within me.

Psalm 51:10

As we grow older, we seem to have more time to think about some of the really dumb things we have done. There are very few of us who have not made some unforgivable choices that affected other people—maybe our families, friends, or others with whom we worked.

Perhaps we could not bring ourselves to go to a friend who had experienced profound grief. At the time we rationalized with many excuses. Or maybe we talked too much to others about something that was a private matter to someone else. Or it could be that we just didn't call someone to say "Hello."

Some of the choices have been on our conscience for many years. We may need to talk with a Christian counselor or a respected clergy member about those choices. Sometimes we just need to talk with God and tell him how we feel. He alone forgives us for the many acts of injustice that we know we have done. What a wonderful, loving God to show his love to us in this way.

Every day, by the grace of God, we begin a new life, following the example of our Lord and Savior, Jesus Christ. He gives us the strength and forgiveness to begin a new life daily.

Dear God,
You are the God who knows all of our shortcomings. We need you to hear us as we think about wrongs we have done to others. With your help we will try to do what you would have us do. Amen.

Be Not Afraid

Perfect love casts out all fear.
        1 John 4:18

Everyone has fears of some kind or another and our fears change as we get older. What frightens some of us the most is the thought that there will not be enough money to function independently. We may also be concerned about our health or the health of someone close to us. What happens if we don't have the money to pay for extended care or a nursing home?

The newspaper gives us more to fear. Every day we read about horrible murders, senseless explosions, floodwaters, earthquakes, airplane malfunctions, hurricanes, or robberies. Have you ever wondered how the people who were killed in such tragedies dealt with their fear? What would we do if we were in the same situation?

Someone close to me is going through the fear of what diagnostic tests will reveal about cancer. He knows he has prostate cancer now. Several years ago he had a more serious cancer operation. Of course he is scared, and waiting to hear the diagnosis seems to take forever. However, he trusts in the Lord and is trying to be patient.

It is not wrong to have fears. When we are frightened, telling people what is bothering us always seems to help. They may share with us about how they overcome their anxieties. We also need to tell God our fears and put our trust in him. He will always be with us.

Dear God,
Help us to put our love and trust in you. Sometimes we are afraid, and we don't know what to do. We know that you will be there with us at those times. Thank you for your love and concern. Amen.

Are You Happy?

Happy are the people who trust in the LORD.
                                        Proverbs 16:20

Just what makes us happy? Having good fortune on the stock market? Living in a beautiful debt-free home? Having family nearby who frequently surprise us by stopping in for a visit? Or even seeing old friends from decades back? Maybe it is knowing that we are alive and moving each new day.

Certainly those things make us happy, and of course we have other days when unfortunate events happen and we are sad. But even in sadness we can be happy, knowing that God shares our sadness and our happiness. When we think about the many times we bring sorrow to God, we can also think about how, even so, he brings happiness to us. That's what our loving God does.

Sometimes we can tell from the look on a person's face if he or she is happy. Recently, at a meeting, I noticed how very sad one of the group members looked. I missed the cheerfulness he usually displayed. Since I was worried, I called him the next day. He was so grateful to know that someone was concerned. I learned that this person had good reason to look sad—that he needed the prayers of our group.

There is a children's song that tells them to clap their hands, stomp their feet, and shout "Hooray!" if they are happy. Do we need to clap our hands as we think about the many times God has made us happy? How does he use us in giving others happiness? Without God we would not know real happiness.

Dear God,
You are our greatest source of happiness. Help us to show others our happiness. We are happy to be having a love affair with you. Amen.

Are You Weary?

"Come to me, all you who are weary and carrying heavy burdens, and I will give you rest."

Matthew 11:28

Sometimes it's difficult to figure out why we get weary when it seems we haven't accomplished anything. How can this be? We wear ourselves out trying to help others who are lonely, in pain, or unhappy with their children's lives, and we see no change in what is happening to these people. At times, we become discouraged with our own lives, when things don't go as planned. We were so sure that, as we grew older, our burdens would be lighter to carry.

When we are both emotionally and physically weary, it is time to tell God our burdens. Many spouses who have given care to their mate for a number of years are completely drained by the time their loved one dies. The husband of a friend recently died after several years of special care. My friend told that she is helping a blind friend move to another home. She misses her husband very much, but she does not feel so tired. What a wonderful God to help my friend help others.

If we make a greater effort to tell God our burdens, he will help us. He has told us that his yoke is easy and his burden light, and that we must not weary of doing what is right (Matt. 11:30, Gal. 6:9). Our beloved God is there for us, and he will share our burdens when we need him. We must not be afraid to ask for his help.

Dear God,
We look to you for help when we have concerns about others or when our lives seem filled with unhappiness. Many times we become weary, but we known that you alone will give us the rest we need when we ask for your help. Amen.

Forgiveness

Be kind to one another, tenderhearted, forgiving one another, as God in Christ has forgiven you.

Ephesians 4:32

In order to continue our love affair with God, we must be able to forgive those who have done upsetting things to us. I think about how God forgives us for forgetting to put him first in our lives. God also forgives us when we neglect to give him thanks for all of his blessings. Our heavenly love affair with God does not mean that we never need to be forgiven or that we never need to forgive.

We are probably aware of many things for which we need to be forgiven. Perhaps there are family situations in which we did not act in a godly manner. Have you ever thought about how sad God must be when family members cannot forgive each other? It would be a heavenly gift if all the families on earth were in harmony.

Do you know of any situations in which it would have been better not to have said the unkind word? Even as we ask for forgiveness, we know that God has forgiven us for all of our wrongdoings. Let us be aware of his love and forgive all of those who have hurt us. We would not be having such a wonderful love affair if God were not forgiving.

Dear God,
Help us to be kind to one another, tenderhearted, and forgiving. We ask you to help us avoid being so judgmental of other people and their situations. We thank you for your forgiveness of our sins. Amen.

Love Your Neighbor as Yourself

Love does no wrong to a neighbor.
Romans 13:10

The Bible tells us to love our neighbors, but sometimes we never even see who lives nearby. Because of the many demands that our neighbors may have from their jobs and families or from their various other activities, we may never get to see or know them. It seems that the concept of neighborhoods, as we remember them, is fast disappearing. However, that should not keep us from loving our neighbors.

It is difficult to love our neighbors at times, especially when we have had a disagreement on some neighborhood concern. This often happens when a homeless shelter of some sort or a soup kitchen wants to locate in the vicinity. Establishments such as recovery homes can cause controversy. Do we give thought to what God would want us to do? Do we think about the real reasons we may be opposed to certain plans? Do we love our neighbors as ourselves?

Not too long ago, on a very hot day, I saw a man sitting in our front yard. I watched as he rolled over and started to crawl. When I approached him, he wasn't able to tell me who he was or where he lived. I called the police for help and they arrived within minutes. I shall never forget how kind they were to the man. He was a victim of Alzheimer's disease and had no idea where he was. I am sure those young policeman were sharing God's love. And I hope that everyone who stopped to watch will share his or her love with any neighbors who need help.

Dear God,
You are so loving to all, regardless of where they live or what they believe. Sometimes it is difficult for us to love our neighbors, and we need your help to overcome our failures in this area. Thank you for being our favorite neighbor. Amen.

Fellowship

"For where two or three are gathered in my name, I am there among them."

Matthew 18:20

Most churches have a coffee hour after services, which gives worshipers a chance to get to know others. Often, however, it is hard for people to attend a coffee hour, especially if they are shy, new to the church, or just visiting. But many find that the coffee hour satisfies their need to have fellowship with others. Sometimes, as we grow older and retire, we don't have as many chances to be with people. Not only can one find fellowship at church with other people, but one can also find fellowship with God.

I am sure that God wants all of us in the world to come together in love. How important it becomes, then, for churches to have comradeship with other churches in their area or in the country. We can become partners with churches in other lands and learn more about their ways of worshiping. Think of the friendliness among members during denominational conventions. There is never complete agreement on issues, but there is fellowship with others and with God. We know that our loving God is the reason we enjoy being with others.

Dear God,
We know that you are always with us when we come together with others to do your work. Help us to remember that through fellowship we will become closer to you. Amen.

Is Your Light Turned On?

Let your light shine before others, so that they may see your good works and give glory to your Father in heaven.
Matthew 5:16

When I first attended the church where I later became a member, I thought the words above, said before the offering was taken, were wonderful. I still think so. What a challenge God has given to us. Think about how your life shines and shows the glory of God. Maybe you shine with a smile, the touch of a hand, a phone call, a kind word, or through singing in the church choir, teaching Sunday school, or being a loving and caring person to your mate or to a dear friend.

When you are in a group of people at a meeting, in church, or even at a grocery store, it is easy to notice the shining lights of different individuals. There is something different about them. When we think of God and the life of Jesus, it is easy to see that his light shone everywhere he went. How lucky we are to be having a love affair with someone so special. Every day think about how your light shines, and think of ways to make it even brighter.

Dear God,
We thank you for giving us your son, Jesus—the light of the world. We know that some days our light does not shine too brightly. We need your help to think about ways our light can reflect our love of you. Amen.

Anger

Whoever is slow to anger has great understanding, but one who has a hasty temper exalts folly.

Proverbs 14:29

There is no one alive who does not have some anger inside of him or her. Even Jesus showed his anger in the temple. As we grow older, we hope that we have learned to avoid being angry about things God would consider trivial. Anger can hurt others and cause people discomfort.

We need to remember that God wants us to be slow to anger. By taking time to think, we can better understand situations that may provoke us. Our anger might surface when others make remarks we don't like. Maybe we don't like what is happening in the world today. Or maybe we just feel like arguing, and then we lose our tempers. Let's try to put all of those feelings into God's hands and ask for his help.

God is a loving God. He wants us to be loving, too. Being angry takes a lot out of us, and we cannot do his work if we are irritated. When we are angry, however, we can use our anger in healthy ways. I seem to get rid of much of my anger if I busy myself by working in the yard or cleaning in the house. Sometimes writing letters to friends will help. Walking or participating in sports can also help to calm us down. We have been told not to let the sun go down on our anger. (Eph. 4:26). That is wonderful advice.

Dear God,
Sometimes we get angry. Sometimes we are angry with you, for no reason.
Please forgive us as we learn to be more patient. Amen.

Gifts

Now there are a variety of gifts, but the same Spirit.
1 Corinthians 12:4

As our love affair continues, we are overwhelmed with the many gifts God has given to us. God must certainly think we are deserving. It is up to us to use these gifts to show his love to others in the world.

Our gifts are unique. Some people have musical abilities; some are able to make others feel good about themselves. Teachers share their gifts with students. Ministers have special talents, as do physicians, nurses, and all people who work in the healthcare field. It doesn't matter if we are writers, engineers, scientists, clerical workers, or carpenters. Neither our occupation nor our age makes any difference. We all have received special gifts from God.

How can any of these gifts be used to spread the Word of God to show his love to others? Are some gifts more valuable than others? Do our gifts change during our lifetime? How do we know where our gifts are needed the most?

As it says in 1 Peter 4:10, "Like good stewards of the manifold grace of God, serve one another with whatever gift each of you has received." How wonderful it would be to share God's love with everyone.

Most gracious God,
Thank you for the wonderful gifts you have given us. Help us to use them to glorify your name. Amen.

Faith of Our Fathers

Now faith is the assurance of things hoped for, the conviction of things not seen.

Hebrews 11:1

It is difficult to tell someone about our faith. Words to describe our faith elude us, and it is something we just seem to know. We know that we trust the Lord, as did many others whose stories are told in the Bible. Think of Noah as he loaded the ark and later as he waited for dry land to appear. Think of Abraham when he sacrificed his son Isaac as an offering. What faith they had. There are many instances when Jesus told individuals whom he had healed that their faith had saved them.

I think it is very important to show our faith by what we do in times of trouble *and* in times of joy. If we trust God, this is not hard to do. He will never let us down. There is no question in my mind that my faith and that of my husband kept me alive through some unexpected surgery. And when we talked about moving to Florida, many of our friends laughed—they were sure we wouldn't stay. But we had faith in our decision, and it turned out to be the right one. How many times has your faith seen you through difficult situations?

How much stronger our faith will become as we walk hand in hand with our heavenly Father. Let's pray that our faith will be an example to others, to draw closer to God.

Dear God,
We know we need to show others how much you mean to us by living a godly and righteous life. We pray that you will help us show our faith to others. Amen.

Let There Be Peace

"Peace I leave with you; my peace I give to you."
                                                    John 14:27

Doesn't it seem as if it's taking a long time for God to answer our prayers for peace? We have seen so many wars in our life. Fighting and killing are still going on all over the world. But as we grow older, we become concerned about another kind of peace—the peace inside of us.

So many people lack inner peace. Families today face the problems of drugs, unwanted pregnancy, alcoholism, divorce, AIDS, and other difficulties. We, too, face many difficulties as we age. We are very apt to be forgetful, which is disturbing. We find that it takes us longer to do everyday tasks. And coping with serious health problems is not easy.

My husband's aging mother lives in a nursing home hundreds of miles away from us. We are not able to visit her often, but when we do make our yearly visit, we always feel better. Seeing her so well taken care of helps us to have inner peace.

Jesus told us not to be troubled or afraid (John 14:27). When we are upset, we need to let God know about our adversities. He will hear our prayers, and we will begin to feel the inner peace that only God can give us. Philippians 4:7 says, "And the peace of God, which surpasses all understanding, will guard your hearts and your minds in Christ Jesus." What more do we need?

Dear God,
We know that inner peace comes only from you. When we are discouraged we will try to remember that you are beside us. Thank you for your promise of peace. Amen.

Sharing

They are to do good, to be rich in good works, generous and ready to share.

1 Timothy 6:18

We learned most of our lessons in sharing when we were youngsters at home. During the Depression, we had to share food, clothes, toys, our homes, and many other things. I have never forgotten the sad feeling I had when our Sunday school had a drive to collect toys. I was under six years old and someone had given me a drum. I loved that drum, but I was able to be agreeable and share it with someone else. (I'm sure my parents were glad I did.)

As we have grown older, many of us have had several more experiences in sharing our possessions. When someone we knew needed something to help him or her through a crisis, everyone shared his or her belongings with the person. I remember a lavender coat I wore until I outgrew it. For years afterward, that coat was seen in many parts of Ohio. Often churches had drives to collect items for disaster victims. These acts of sharing are ongoing today.

With God's help we are learning to share in different ways. Take time to think about the many ways you can give of yourself to others. Each of us has many talents just waiting to be shared with people we see every day. Our sense of humor or our wisdom can bring joy to many people. But most of all, we need to share God with others.

Dear God,
We are so thankful that our love for you has grown. We want to be able to share what we have so that others may know of your wonderful love. You have been so wonderful to share your love with us. Thank you. Amen.

Do You Have a Mission?

"The harvest is plentiful, but the laborers are few."
                                        Matthew 9:37

I believe that God has given each of us a mission. Part of that mission is to share God's word and love with others. The harvest is still plentiful, but it seems there aren't many workers.

When I was a child, it seemed that in church we heard a lot about missionaries. And when I began to do Christian education work, inviting a missionary to speak to the children was exciting. Later in my life, however, that term didn't seem to be in use. Now, though, we are again hearing about mission frequently. In fact, I heard three women talking to a group about their missionary work in three countries. Their stories were told with such joy that it was easy to see how much they enjoyed laboring for the Lord.

We are in the harvest of our lives. Recently a bishop told us that the churches should not be retirement centers. That puts us in a dilemma, however. How can we older people bring younger people into our church? How can we be missionaries at this time in our lives?

Do we need to get expert advice from younger church leaders? There are many missionary societies ready to help us sort out our priorities. And if we give our concerns to God, we will know our mission. Let's be ready to help gather in the harvest.

Dear God,
We put our lives into your wonderful hands. Show us how we can be missionaries for you in today's world. Amen.

Where Is Your Treasure?

"For where your treasure is, there your heart will be also."
Matthew 6:21

The words of Jesus clearly tell us that the most important things in our lives are those things that we love the most. Did you ever give priorities to your treasures? Is owning a high-priced car on your list? How about an expensive home in an exclusive area? Money, fancy clothes, a good figure, and an unblemished complexion could be on your list.

There are so many material and other treasures that we could have in our lives. We may never realize that some valued treasures have been with us forever. Our parents are treasures. And so are our spouses and children. Good friends and fond memories of happy times with family are like jewels. Even our education can be a treasure. If we enjoy gardening, the plants that we have nurtured into prize-winning specimens are our pride and joy. My own treasures include all of my family, my church, my friends, my home, and my health. What are your treasures?

There is one treasure I haven't noted. That is God's love. How wonderful it is that we are having a love affair with God. The Bible tells us not to let riches stand in the way of our relationship with him. If we want to inherit eternal life, we must keep our love affair alive.

Dear God,
We have many treasures, but you are the very best. Help us to keep our love affair with you growing. Amen.

When Does One Retire?

All must test their own work; then that work, rather than their neighbor's work, will become a cause for pride.

Galatians 6:4

Retirement. Forty or fifty years ago we thought retirement was just for old people. Now that we are getting close to the age of retirement, or have already retired, we realize we were mistaken. We certainly are not old, and we have the option and ability to do so many different things.

When I retired from teaching I missed the children. Then God gave me the opportunity to teach preschool. From there I became a Christian education coordinator. Upon finishing in this role I decided to retire for good, but I did some consultant work, helping churches with their Christian education programs. Furthermore, I am still writing. God has been with me as I write, so I am sure I will never retire as long as I allow him to help me.

The God who has known us forever never retires. And regardless of anything else we do, we should not retire from doing God's work. Even our loved ones and friends who are in nursing homes are not retired from doing his work. They teach us to be patient, kind, and thankful for every moment of life we have had and every moment of life yet to come.

The words of the hymn "Come Labor On" urge us to keep working until our days on earth are done. There are many ways to labor for God—any work we do can be for his glory.

Dear God,
Give us the strength to labor on for you. We are your servants. Help us to do your work for the rest of our days on earth. We love you. Amen.

Mountains

I lift up my eyes to the hills—from where will my help come?
Psalm 121:1

Although I have never lived near mountains, I have always thought
of them as one of God's wondrous works. As a youngster I loved
to visit my grandmother who did live in a town surrounded by mountains. (The Bible verse above quickly became one of my favorites.)

Not too long ago my husband and I were driving through those
same mountains during our vacation. Of course they are not as lofty
as I remembered them, but they still give me a wonderful feeling.
One morning, while we were driving, it was very foggy and it was
difficult to even follow the road. Then, all of a sudden, the fog was
gone. This happened several times that morning.

I was reminded that we all have fog in our lives. We blunder
along at times, now knowing in what direction we want our lives to

go. Suddenly, we hear what God is telling us. The fog has been lifted, but we know it will return another time. At those times in life our help comes from the Lord.

Do you think Jesus looked up to the hills asking for God's help? He often went by himself into the mountains to pray. Where was he when he chose his disciples? Where was he when he delivered the Beatitudes?

All of us have mountains and valleys in our lives. If we didn't have some valleys, we would not know the wonder of the mountains. Can you think of the times when God helped you through some bleak valleys?

Dear God,
We know that our help comes from you. You are like a lofty mountain to us and we thank you for being there for us. You have always helped us to find our way out of the valleys. We praise you for your goodness. Amen.

Prejudice

"Love your neighbor as yourself."
                    Romans 13:9

When I was doing Christian education work I always told the teachers about an old hymn I learned as a child: "We've a Story to Tell to the Nations." It told about Christ's kingdom of truth and righteousness coming to earth. I would point out to the teachers that it didn't seem like the story had been told very well. All one needs to do is glance at the daily newspaper and read about the racism and hatred that still goes on all over the world. Almost every day we read about racial violence somewhere in the United States. It seems that we need to tell the story over and over, and perhaps we must learn to tell it in new and different ways.

At times it is difficult for us to accept differences in people. Let us do our best to overcome our own prejudices as we remember that God is never prejudiced. In what new ways can we tell the story and rid ourselves of our prejudices.

Dear God,
Help each one of us to remember your beautiful words: "You shall love your neighbor as yourself." Direct us as we try to tell the whole world about your wonderful love. Amen.

New Directions

"For truly I tell you, if you have faith the size of a mustard seed, you will say to this mountain, 'move from here to there,' and it will move; and nothing will be impossible for you."
Matthew 17:20

Now that we are in our sixties or seventies, or even in our eighties, we have many decisions to make concerning what is best for our individual family situations. Sometimes we know we should move to a smaller home, yet the thought of putting away old memories is overwhelming. The thought of our grandchildren never getting to play where their parents did is upsetting. How much easier it is to stay put and try to keep things going without any change.

In addition to having to make tough decisions it is bothersome to know that a career is coming to an end and that it is time for retirement. Or sometimes our physicians suggest we change the way we are living; serious health problems call for new directions. Do we really want to move to a warmer climate? Are there alternatives to residing in an assisted-living facility? Often we think it is less different to just bury our heads than to think about new directions for our lives.

If we have faith, nothing is impossible. It is best to look at the positive side of a situation when our lives take on new directions. Think of the many people you know who have done just that, and their lives moved forward with God there beside them. What are the wonderful new possibilities that might await you if you move forward, in a new direction?

Dear God,
Help us to make wise decisions concerning changes in our lives. We want to show our faith in you as our lives take us in unknown directions. Amen.

Worry

"So do not worry about tomorrow, for tomorrow will bring worries of its own. Today's trouble is enough for today."
Matthew 6:34

We have all been told that we should put any problems that worry us into God's hands. It is very easy to say those words, but for many of us, it is a difficult thing to do. We like to be in control of things; however, as we grow older, we find that we don't always have control.

Often I agonize and pray about something I am worried about. I wake up during the night agonizing. After a couple of days I find I am no longer concerned. I know that God has helped me.

Sometimes we need to focus on happenings other than our own worries. If we live day by day, our troubles will be much easier to handle. And, if of course, we need to talk to God about what is bothering us. We may find that a quiet time helps us to think about solutions to our concerns. We can be ready for any outcome if we let God, the most wonderful God, come into our lives and help us.

Take time to think about the many times you were worried and God stood beside you. How has he helped you through difficult times in your past?

Dear God, who shares all our worries,
Help us to put our faith and trust in you. We will try to place more of our problems into your hands so that you can help us. Amen.

Joy

O come, let us sing to the LORD; let us make a joyful noise to the Rock of our salvation.

Psalm 95:1

How wonderful this love affair is! I can't carry a tune, but every morning I want to sing with joy, just because I am alive. Besides, I am sure that God doesn't mind if I can't carry a tune, although I was nearly prevented from becoming a teacher because of that. But since I played the piano, I was allowed to teach. Wherever I taught you could always hear my class singing. It was wonderful to be around the children and to see the joy on their faces when they sang.

There seems to be a trend in some worship services, with the congregation expressing its joy in new ways. There may be clapping and foot stomping. Or there may be guitar music and dancing. Perhaps clowns are part of the worship service. These newer ways may seem unsettling to us, but the love affair we have with God helps us to express our joy in our own special ways.

Let us look for joy in the faces of the people we see daily. If we can't detect it, then, perhaps, with God's help we can bring joy to them.

Dear God,
Sometimes we feel that there is no joy in the world, but all we need to do is take time to feel your love in our lives. We are joyful that you love us. Amen.

Are You Listening?

"Let anyone with ears listen."
Matthew 11:15

Sometimes I wonder if we ever really do listen to God. It seems to me that he is always telling us something, if we would just open our ears to hear. This is true of individuals and groups of people throughout the world—just a glance at the paper confirms this. When I see people doing their daily exercises while listening to an electronic device, I wonder if they hear anything at all. But then, it doesn't really matter where one is. God speaks to us anywhere. He surely must speak to those people wearing headsets, too.

The world is full of God's sounds and words for us. I love to walk along the beach and hear the waves coming into the shore and the seabirds making all kinds of noise. If you walk in the woods, you can hear God in the quietness of the trees. Sitting on a log, you can hear the beautiful sounds of the streams, the birds, the wind, and even of silence. If you are in the city, you can hear the sounds of it waking up.

Wherever you are, you can hear God. Make time to listen to him and your love affair will continue to grow.

Dear God,
We know we need to listen to you, but it isn't always easy. We ask you to help us hear what you are telling us every minute of every day. Amen.

God's Creation

God saw everything that he had made, and indeed, it was very good.

Genesis 1:31

When I see so many of God's creations all around me, I want to sing praises to God. Just being able to be outdoors and to see so many of his creations is a blessing. As I walk or ride my bike in the morning, I see the moon's light fade as the sun rises. The changes in the skies, the trees, the flowers, the ponds, and the whole landscape, as I ride by, are wonderful to behold.

Then, as I walk beside the Gulf of Mexico and hear the sounds of the birds and the water, my mind is swept clear of mundane things. I think of our heavenly Father's greatness in creating so many different sea animals. To see a glimpse of a colorful coquina or to find a sea horse is still a thrill. I see shells that once had living creatures in them, and I think about how different each one is. Each is unique, just as we are.

Think about the hymn "All Things Bright and Beautiful" and make a mental list every day of the bright and beautiful things you see.

Dear God,
We are thankful to you for creating such a beautiful world. Help us to preserve all of the beauty you have shown us. Be with us as we continue our love affair with you. Amen.

Love

You shall love the LORD your God with all your heart, and with all your soul, and with all your might.

Deuteronomy 6:5

One of the first Bible verses we learned as children was "God is love" (1 John 4:16). Is it any surprise to you—now that you are over sixty—that you are having a heavenly love affair? Of course the love affair is with God, who already loves us more than we can ever comprehend. Every day I try to think about all of the ways God has shown love for me. I try to take time to pray that this affair continues for ever and ever. It is so easy, however, to put other activities ahead of this time to reflect and pray.

I have been told that if one puts aside fifteen minutes for personal devotion, ten minutes must be in complete silence and the other five minutes in prayer. Recently, a friend told me she was bothered with the idea of having ten minutes of silence during her devotional time. I suggested to her that by our silence we invite God to enter our lives. As we listen in silence, we become more aware of how God shows us his love. How heavenly it is to become more aware of God in our lives.

Dear God,
Open our minds to behold all of your love. Be with us as we pray that your heavenly love will be shown to everyone throughout the world. Amen.

Prayer

"Hear my prayer, O LORD, and give ear to my cry."
Psalm 39:12

As our heavenly love affair grows, it helps to take time to recall those instances when prayer helped us to overcome some difficulty. This is not always easy to do, because many times our very breath is a continual prayer. Furthermore, we do not always know when friends are praying for us. We may ask a special friend to keep us in his or her prayers for a specific purpose; that friend may ask another friend to pray for us; and the chain of prayer goes on and on, unknown to us.

It is important, to me, to reach out to others who are in need of prayer. I like to remember the people who are sad and mistreated—those whom I read about in the daily paper or see on television.

Still, there are so many people in need of prayer. Sometimes it seems that we don't have enough hours in the day to pray for everyone. A friend of mine has a solution to this. She sends up "dart" prayers during the day and night. Anytime she thinks of someone in need of prayer (aren't we all?) she sends up a prayer. What an easy thing to do as we think of people throughout the day.

God hears all of our prayers. How wonderful it is to be having a love affair with him.

Dear God,
We offer you prayers for all of our friends in this wonderful world you have made. Help us to especially remember the people in the world who are suffering. Amen.

Changes

"For I the LORD do not change."
Malachi 3:6

All of God's creations change—trees, flowers, vegetables, the sky, the sea, each one of us. Our bodies undergo change as we age, but we can still remain beautiful, inspiring, and reassuring to our children, grandchildren, and friends.

Some of us find it difficult to accept the changes in our world as we grow older. We have had to learn new terminology and different methods of worshiping. We can't stand modern music, and it is difficult to accept today's values and morals. I am sure that God does not want us to give up our morals, values, and worshiping habits just because it appears that the world around us has done so.

Instead of dwelling on those changes that are difficult to accept, we need to keep focused on the good changes in the world, for there are many. Every day we can read about new advances in medicine. We have many conveniences we didn't have before. We are able to take care of most of our business by using a touch-tone telephone. We never have to go inside a bank to get spending money anymore.

If we ask God to help us accept some of the new ideas, perhaps our lives will be easier and happier. May we always remember that there is one thing that never changes—God's love for us.

Gracious God,
You know all of our shortcomings. We need your help to make good changes in our lives. Make known to us how we can change to follow you better.
Amen.

Death

"I am the resurrection and the life. Those who believe in me, even though they die, will live, and everyone who lives and believes in me will never die."

John 11:25–26

Death is one of the things we can be certain of, just as we know we can count on God's love. Each one of us has probably faced the death of a friend or someone in our family. As more and more of our family and friends die, we need to remember that those who believe in Christ never die.

I remember a sermon I heard many years ago. The minister was retired and his wife had died a few weeks before. He said that too many people say someone is "lost" when that person dies. A person might be lost at the shopping mall, he told us, and we might not know where to look for them. But when Christians die, they are *not* lost, for we know that they are with God.

The book of John in the New Testament has so many comforting words. Reading those words helps to ease the sorrow we experience after the death of a loved one. And as we read the words, we need to remember that from death comes new life.

Almighty God,
Be with us when we mourn the death of someone we love. Help us to follow you so that we will be reunited with loved ones in eternal life. Amen.

God's House

I was glad when they said to me, "Let us go to the house of the LORD."
Psalm 122:1

God has many different church houses. Some are beautiful cathedrals, some are plain structures, and some are even tents. It may be hard to recognize that a structure or an outdoor area is a church because we may not see a cross.

Once, when my husband and I were traveling in New England, we came upon signs leading to an outdoor cathedral. We followed the signs and soon were at a most beautiful scenic setting. In that house of God we were aware of the presence of Christ. Some of our friends travel in their RVs for long periods of time. Although they are on the road, they never miss going to church on Sunday. Every campsite they stay at has outdoor church services. Ministers of mainline denominations preside, and sometimes there is even a choir.

Think about the people in nursing homes who may be worshiping in a chapel or in a dining room. Hospitals have chapels for patients and visitors. Can you think of other places to worship?

Just as the structures vary, so does the music. Some churches have magnificent choirs, organs, orchestras, rock music, bell choirs, or children's choirs—all of them different. It doesn't matter what the house looks like or what music is heard. The people who attend services at these churches are there to praise God together and to hear his word. And that is what matters.

To glorify our loving God in his house is a wonderful privilege. We can share the joy of our heavenly love affair when we worship with others in our own church. Isn't it a blessing that we are still able to be a part of a group gathered together to give praise to the Lord?

Dear God,
We are thankful that we can still give praise to you in your house. Help us to feel comfort, fellowship, peace, and security as we share your love with others. Amen.

Friends

A friend loves at all times.
Proverbs 17:17

For the past seventeen years I have enjoyed walking along the beach early in the morning. Now that I am retired, I enjoy walking with my husband, who is my best friend. I have spoken to many people as I have walked. I do not know all of their names, but they are my friends. If I don't see those people, I become concerned. It is a relief when I see them walking again.

Friends are special people who add happiness to our lives. They accept us just as we are, and never try to change us. They remain loyal to us even when we have adversities. We, in turn, are loving and loyal to them.

Have you ever noticed how God has brought new friends into our lives just when we needed them? Maybe he brought a friend who will listen to us as we think aloud. Or maybe it was someone who adds humor to our lives. Perhaps he brought us a very special person to love. Think about how blessed we are to have a love affair with the best friend of all, God.

Dear God,
What a friend you are. We call on you again and again to listen to us and to guide us. We are thankful for all of the friends we have met through you. We will try to follow your example and be loving friends to them. We give thanks that you are our best friend. Amen.

Heartaches

I have great sorrow and unceasing anguish in my heart.
Romans 9:2

Each of us has encountered many heartaches during our lifetime. The untimely death of a loved one, a family disagreement that cannot be healed, divorce, or a terminal illness can all cause anguish in our hearts. When our son was found dead, the heartache my husband and I experienced was awful. But that loving God of ours was with us and somehow helped us to heal as the days and months went on. I cannot imagine how we would have gotten through that time of our lives if God had not been a part of our life together. I often think of the mother of Jesus and the grief she must have experienced as Jesus was crucified.

It is important to remember that God is always with us, when we are happy or when we are sad. Sometimes his comfort may come through others who are able to strengthen us as we cry and pray together. Just a touch of a friend's hand can do wonders for someone who is enduring heartache. It is God's love that makes us happy and whole again.

Dear God,
As our love affair grows with you, we know that you are always with us and will heal our anguish. What a wonderful God you are, and we pray that we can show your love to others who may be suffering great sorrow. Amen.

Patience

May you be made strong with all the strength that comes from his glorious power, and may you be prepared to endure everything with patience.

Colossians 1:11

As we grow older, it is sometimes easier to be patient because we have had a great deal of experience in patience. As we faced upheavals in our lives, we learned that things would always work out in God's good time. On the other hand, there are many times when we feel that we have no patience at all.

Think about the frustrating encounters that face us today. Here in Florida driving during the tourist season is a harrowing event. During Advent I once heard a sermon that acknowledged how long one had to wait at certain traffic lights. The minister compared that long period of waiting to the time of waiting for Christ to come as we go through the season of Advent.

Do you ever think that God might be impatient with us, just as he probably was with the people in the Old Testament who were waiting for the Messiah? How many times have you been restless waiting for an answer from God? Let us never forget that love is patient and kind.

Dear God,
We humbly thank you for being patient with us throughout our lives. We are truly sorry for the many times when we were not patient with you. Thank you for loving us. Amen.

Let the Children Come to Me

"Let the children come to me, and do not stop them; for it is to such as these that the kingdom of heaven belongs."
Matthew 19:14

When we observe some of today's children it is very difficult for us to remain happy and cheerful. Sometimes their clothes, their attitudes, their music, and even their joyful sounds can annoy us. I recall a friend complaining about a high school–age girl who had worn an old pair of jeans to church. The girl had not been in church for many months, so I reminded my friend that we should not pass judgment on her but instead rejoice that she was worshiping with her mother and sisters.

Most people our age get very upset when children talk in church. When we were youngsters, we learned to be quiet in church. Giving the kids dirty looks is not the answer. Since our hearing is not as good as it used to be, maybe we should sit closer to the front of the church. Then we can concentrate on what is being said from the pulpit.

Remember when we were young and we went through a world war and a Depression? Young people of today also go through many disturbing things. Let us be accepting and loving of them as they search for meaning in their lives, just as God is loving and accepting of all of his children.

Dear God,
Help us to always create a loving and caring environment for all of your children, young or old. We want to be able to show your love to each child of yours. Amen.

Judgment

"Why do you see the speck in your neighbors' eye, but do not notice the log in your own eye?"

Matthew 7:3

A s we grow older, it seems as if sometimes we feel very sure that our viewpoints and ways of doing things are the only right ones. We probably pass judgment on any views that are not similar to our own. Maybe we are even defensive about our thoughts on any subject.

Sometimes the specks in our neighbors' eyes seem to shine more brightly than the logs in our own eyes. It is then that we need to see things in a different light. A friend of mine told me she often needs to have long talks with herself to help her see if her way of thinking really makes sense. I find that I also have that need. These talks are really conversations with God. He helps us to see all sides of an issue more clearly.

We need to be sure that our thoughts are not prejudiced, except those about God's eternal love. He can help us overcome the logs in our eyes so that we can continue our wonderful love affair with him.

Dear God,
We know that we are being unfair when we don't want to listen to the opinion of someone else. Help us to be more open and tolerant, and to know when to speak and when to be still. We need your help every minute of every day and night. We never want this heavenly love affair to end. Amen.

Unexpected Events

Rejoice in hope, be patient in suffering, persevere in prayer.
Romans 12:12

Every family is confronted with unexpected happenings from time to time. Sometimes difficult times just can't be avoided. The death of loved ones or good friends can be devastating. Being told by your physician that you need surgery or more tests to determine the extent of your illness can throw a wrench into your plans. Even facing the fact that a young doctor has replaced the doctor you've known for years can be upsetting.

I am sure that you can think of many things that are upsetting to you. How do we cope? I remember my mother saying "Gird up your loins," and I often find myself repeating that Bible verse (Job 38:3). We are having a love affair with God, and he will be with us during all of our trials and tribulations. When we are struggling, it may not seem that he is there. But as we look back at situations, we know in our hearts that God was there as we stumbled along. How wonderful it is to have a God who loves each one of us.

Dear God,
You are our fortress when the unexpected happens. We thank you for being present when we need guidance. Amen.

What Can I Give Him?

"It is more blessed to give than to receive."
Acts 20:35

God has been so wonderful to us, and it is a great joy to give back to him all we can. Sometimes we think giving involves only money. Let's think about the many other ways we can give of ourselves to God.

We have been told to do good, to be generous with our possessions and deeds, and to share with others. Each of us has many gifts, special skills that we alone possess. Now is the time to use those skills to serve God.

Greeting someone with a handicap is a way we can give of ourselves. By taking time to pray for others in distress we are contributing to God's work. If we sing in the choir or teach Sunday school, we share our skills. Volunteering our time to some project at our church or in the community is another way to give. When we smile at children and give them a compliment we are sharing a little of God's love.

What are your special gifts? What can you contribute to this heavenly love affair?

Dear God,
We can never give to you as much as you give to us. Help us share with others the skills you have given us. Help us to be more generous in every way possible. Help us to know you better. Amen.

Heavenly Heavens

The heavens are telling the glory of God.
Psalm 19:1

Think about how full the heavens are of many different, glorious spectacles. During the day or night the sky may be noisy with airplanes as they make their way to different parts of the world. And now, as never before, we are aware of travel in space. Sometimes we are able to see a satellite orbiting the earth. Hearing a sonic boom as a space shuttle prepares for landing is a glorious sound. Behind the activity, however, we may see the sun or the clouds during the day. And at night, if it is dark and clear, we can see hundreds of stars and the moon.

The sky is full of wonderful metaphors for our lives. The beautiful, fluffy clouds that add such glory to the heavens could quickly become storm clouds, warning us of heavy rain, tornadoes, or hurricanes. After a storm we look for a rainbow to appear as a reminder of God's promise to his people. And we can think of the stars as God's countless blessings to us. Many times our lives become clouded or like falling stars. With God's help, we are lifted up and the brightness in our lives is restored.

What a glorious, loving God we have to share his heavenly heavens with us.

Dear God,
We thank you for all of the glorious things we see in the heavens. When we look upward, we will think of your glorious works and know that you are with us forever in this life, and in the next. Amen.

What Am I Doing Here?

Make me know your ways, O LORD; teach me your paths.
Psalm 25:4

Recently I have heard several younger people wonder what is their purpose in life. I have never questioned why I am here, because I have always known that God will use me wherever I can do the most good. However, I am sure that in my youth the meaning of life was not as clear or as sharp as it is now.

Recall your past and think of the many instances you just happened to see someone who needed his or her spirits lifted. How many different people have you helped during a sorrowful or difficult time in their life? Have you ever thought about why you took certain positions or traveled to different places? Could it be that God really does have a plan for us?

God's role in our lives has always been wonderful. Let's continue to share his love with others and serve him wherever we are. Our love affair with God grows as we learn about God's plan for us and become closer to him.

Dear God,
We know that we are here to share your love with others. We ask for your help in loving, encouraging, and listening to the people we are with daily. We are thankful for the love affair we have with you. Amen.

Where He Leads Me, I Will Follow

"I am the light of the world. Whoever follows me will never walk in darkness but will have the light of life."
                                                              John 8:12

What comforting words from John. But as we grow older, we find it is very difficult to follow Jesus. Sometimes we just want to sit and relax and do nothing. I have found that those times are the best ones in which to think about following Jesus.

The most important way we can imitate Jesus, it seems to me, is to love. It is really quite easy to show our love and follow Jesus. We can do volunteer work, or perhaps make new people feel comfortable and welcomed in our churches. Maybe we can write letters or make phone calls to keep in touch with friends, especially ones going through a difficult period.

There are times when people just need someone to listen to them, times when we need to call a special person so that he or she knows we care. Let's take time to listen to Jesus and be prepared to follow Him with love.

Dear God,
We ask your blessing on us while we continue trying to show your love to others. We know that you always lead us if we take time to listen. We will try to follow you every day. Amen.

Advent: Prepare the Way

"Beware, keep alert; for you do not know when the time will come."
Mark 13:33

Advent is here and we think of the coming of Christ. Soon it will be time for us to celebrate his birthday. We don't know when Christ will come again. We are told to be patient and to keep alert.

Do you remember what it was like when you were a child waiting for Christmas? I could hardly wait for that special day to arrive. There were no televisions to remind us of how many shopping days were left. Shopping was limited because of the Depression, but all of the stores had special decorations. It was a thrill to see the huge tree in one of the downtown establishments in Cleveland. Helping my mother with her special baking projects made the days pass more quickly. Still, when Christmas Eve arrived, it was the longest night of the year.

Waiting is never easy. Have you ever thought about what it was like for the people waiting for the Messiah to come? As we, too, look for Christ, can we ever be as patient as they must have been?

Perhaps we need to look for Christ in the many people who touch our lives. Is it possible that we can see him in a homeless person? Or can we see him in the faces of street children? Do we see him in a friend's smile or handshake? As we wait for Christ to come, let us rejoice.

Dear God,
We are patiently waiting for the day when we will celebrate the birth of your son. Help us to see his face in everyone we come in contact with. We will rejoice as we await the coming observation of Jesus' birth. Amen.

Christmas

The Word became flesh and lived among us, and we have seen his glory.

John 1:14

What a joyful day is Christmas. Just think about what we are celebrating—the birth of Jesus, God's son. If you have an Advent wreath, you know that Advent begins in darkness—no candles are lit. But on Christmas day there are four Advent candles and the Christ candle, all burning brightly. Christ came to bring us light.

We all remember Christmas when we were children. It was such a surprise to receive an unexpected gift. And it was fun to show your friends what you received and to see what they were given. I have often heard people our ages moan that Christmas is for children, and since there are no young children in their family what is the sense of celebrating?

In spite of Christmas gifts, the decorations, Christmas cookies, and the holly and the mistletoe, we know that God, that great God, sent his son to live among us. It doesn't matter if we are young or old, there is still something to celebrate at Christmas.

Think about how the shepherds must have felt when they saw the infant Jesus. Do you think they knew what an impact his birth was going to have on the entire world? At Christmas we are challenged to tell the story of Christ's birth over and over. Then everyone in the world can know of his light and rejoice in his glory.

Dear God,
We think you for giving us the most wonderful gift of all—Jesus Christ. We will rejoice throughout this Christmas season as we celebrate his birth. Amen.

Epiphany: Star of Wonder

When they saw that the star stopped, they were overwhelmed with joy.

Matthew 2:10

During the season of Epiphany we think of a bright star shining in the heavens. Can you imagine a star leading anyone to the birthplace of our Lord and Savior, Jesus Christ? Can you imagine the anticipation in the hearts of those wise men as they followed the star? What joy they must have had as they knelt before the Christ child.

After giving their gifts to the baby Jesus, the wise men were warned in a dream not to tell Herod where the baby was born. They went home a different way. Do you think they knew that Jesus was the light of the world?

Do we follow the light of the world every day? Or do we sometimes take a path that leads away from his light? If we don't follow the star that leads us to Jesus, how will we tell the world about his goodness? Let us rejoice as we follow him.

Most merciful God,
We give thanks for those wonderful wise men who followed the star to Jesus.
We ask you to help us find the right direction to your light. We want everyone in the world to know about you. Amen.

Ash Wednesday

Wash me thoroughly from my iniquity, and cleanse me from my sin.
Psalm 51:2

A sh Wednesday is a solemn day in the church. It is a time to prepare for Lent. Have you ever gone to a Shrove Tuesday pancake supper at a church? Shrove comes from the word shrive, which means "to free from guilt." For many people, Shrove Tuesday simply meant that they could indulge in fatty foods one last time before Lent began. For some of us today, these suppers help set the mood for Ash Wednesday and Lent.

Ash Wednesday is a day of self-examination, reflection, and penance. We all have many sins that bring sorrow to God, us, and others. Can we be freed from our guilt? Are we able to repent? God has promised to forgive us for our wrongdoing if we are truly sorry.

Some of us attend Ash Wednesday services at our church. In some churches the sign of the cross is made on the forehead with ashes from the palms of Palm Sunday. The ashes are a sign of our mortality and penitence. We are reminded that we have everlasting life through Jesus Christ.

Each one of us observes this day a little differently. But we all know that God will forgive us and give us strength. How many times do we reflect on the sorrow we have brought to others? Would it help if we began now, on Ash Wednesday, to think about how we can open our hearts to let God's love enter in?

Dear God,
We confess to you that we have sinned. We ask your forgiveness. Give us courage and strength to follow your ways. We are thankful for your love. Amen.

Lent

He was in the wilderness forty days tempted by Satan.
Mark 1:13

L ent is a good time to think about Jesus in the wilderness. Forty days is a long time to be away from others. It is a long time to be tempted. We have had days, weeks, and even months when we may have been in a wilderness. We were wandering and did not know in which direction we were going. God alone has led us to a better way of living.

Every day we are tempted. Perhaps we have been tempted to tell someone what we really think about him or her. Or we might think it is easier to tell a small lie than to tell the truth. To gossip about someone is tempting at times. Every day we need to examine our daily lives, to look for reasons for our temptations. With God's help they can be overcome.

As we think about the wilderness and temptations during Lent, let's add something to our lives rather than take something away. Could we include extra Bible reading, add a specified prayer time to our busy schedules, or make a commitment to help someone less fortunate than ourselves? We may need to slow down and simplify our lives in order to accomplish any of those things. Then we may be ready to share God's love with everyone we see.

Dear God,
During these days of Lent we will try to add something to our lives to show how much we love you. When we have been in the wilderness and tempted, you have always given us another chance. We thank you for being so loving. Amen.

Holy Week

They went to a place in Gethsemane; and he said to his disciples, "Sit here while I pray."

Mark 14:32

There have been many things for us to think about during Lent, and it is Holy Week. We need to remember what Christ experienced during his last week on earth. His triumphal entry into Jerusalem, the Last Supper with his disciples, Peter's denial, the arrest of Jesus, and the crucifixion are certainly thought-provoking. We know that Jesus suffered.

As we approach Good Friday, Jesus' sufferings can become our sufferings. It sometimes helps to think about each day separately, as we think about the pain Jesus experienced during Holy Week. The most important thing is that we not fall asleep as some of his disciples did. Think about how Jesus must have felt when he returned from praying and found them sleeping.

Many children cannot understand why the day Jesus was crucified is called Good Friday. Many adults don't understand either! Thinking about Christ on the cross makes me very sad, but I know that he suffered so we could have a new life when we die. I know that we will be reunited with our loved ones after our life on earth is over. Now we await the glorious day, Easter Sunday, when we know that Christ rose.

Dear God,
We know that we are not always awake to what you and your son have taught us. We suffer with Jesus during each Lent and feel sorrow on the day he was crucified. Be with us as we try to stay awake and reflect on your most wonderful love. Amen.

Easter: A Celebration

The Lord has risen indeed.
                Luke 24:34

During Lent we gave thought to the last days of Jesus' life on earth. Lent is certainly not the time for celebration, but Easter is different. I call Easter a celebration because we know that the Lord has risen. We know that he has triumphed over death. And because of his victory we know that we will again see our loved ones who have died. What a great comfort that is. It is a glorious gift that God has given to all of us who follow him.

Let's celebrate with great joy on Easter. Can we be joyful in all of our relationships? We will never really understand how much Jesus suffered for us on Good Friday, but we are thankful for what he has given to us. Would we be able to do the same thing for him? Will we be ready for a reunion with God?

Do you ever think about what it must have been like for Mary Magdalene and her friends when they saw that the stone had been rolled away from the tomb? How can we tell the world that Christ the Lord has risen? How long will it take for all the ends of the earth to know about Christ's kingdom?

On Easter morning my husband and I always greet each other before we get out of bed by saying, "The Lord is risen, the Lord is risen indeed. Alleluia, Alleluia." Every day let's celebrate the birth and resurrection of our Lord Jesus. Alleluia, Alleluia.

Dear God,
We give you thanks for the risen Lord as we celebrate his resurrection today. We will be joyful as we think about your wonderful love for us. Amen.

Pentecost: Happy Birthday to the Church

Suddenly from heaven there came a sound like the rush of a violent wind, and it filled the entire house where they were sitting.
Acts 2:2

Many churches observe Pentecost Sunday, the birthday of the church. I have often been involved in celebrating these birthdays. Sometimes congregations are asked to wear red, the color of the Holy Spirit. The children might carry banners. A cake may be decorated in red to also proclaim the birthday.

As we think about Pentecost, we know that is was a very special day. What an awesome experience it must have been for the apostles to receive the gift of the Holy Spirit. They rushed to the streets and preached the good news to anyone who could hear. We are a part of God's church and we, too, have received the Holy Spirit.

Are we doing all we can to tell the world about Jesus Christ? Perhaps we should give thought to new ways to share his love. If we listen to what the Holy Spirit is telling us, we can all spread the good news of Jesus Christ.

Dear God,
We thank you for giving us the gift of the Holy Spirit. Help us to hear what it is telling us. We want to share the good news with the world. Amen.

All Saints' Day

*Praise to the L*ORD*! Sing to the L*ORD *a new song, his praise in the assembly of the faithful.*

Psalm 149:1

This is the day when we pray for all of our loved ones who have died. Although they are not living here on earth, Christ's love brings us together daily. We know that we are in fellowship with all of God's saints, and we will see them in the next life.

Several years ago I was asked to share something about my spiritual journey. I wasn't sure what that meant, so I told how I grew in my knowledge of God. I have no doubt that my spiritual journey was influenced by some saints. These include my grandparents and parents, special clergymen, Sunday school teachers, and many other people who served God. These saints were people who led me in my journey to him. Their love of God was an example to me. From them I learned the importance of loving and serving God. To follow this example daily is a real challenge.

Take time to think about all of the people who are saints in your life. Say a special prayer for each one. Those faithful saints continue to do God's work in heaven. We must carry on his work here on earth.

Dear God,
We give you heartfelt thanks for all of your faithful saints. We hope that we will be able to be in their company in heaven. Amen.